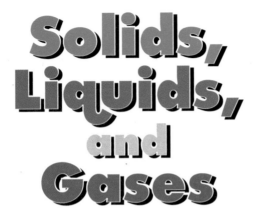

Solids, Liquids, and Gases

written by Mary West

W9-BNA-621

Contents

Solids, Liquids, and Gases 2

Glossary 11

Index 12

Harcourt

Orlando   Boston   Dallas   Chicago   San Diego

www.harcourtschool.com

Today is my dog Frisky's birthday.
We will have a party!

I have balloons for the party. At first the balloons are flat. Then I blow them up.

My breath is a gas. The gas fills each balloon. It takes the shape of the balloon.

I want to have fruit pops at the party.
I pour fruit juice into ice pop molds.
The liquid takes the shape of the molds.

The liquid gets so cold that it turns into a solid. It freezes into hard fruit pops.

Aunt Janie makes a cake for the party.
She beats things in a bowl to make batter.
She mixes up the cake batter until it is
smooth and creamy.

Then she bakes the cake.
Heat makes it change into solid cake.

I wrap Frisky's present. I am giving her a
new dish that has two parts. One part will
hold a liquid and one part will hold a solid.

Frisky can't guess what will go in her dish. Can you?

Glossary

 gas the only form of matter that always fills all the space inside a container

 liquid a form of matter that does not have its own shape

 solid the only form of matter that has a shape of its own

Index

gas, 4
liquid, 5, 6, 9
solid, 6, 8, 9